# A Concise Grammar Book for Those Who Hate Grammar

## STOP MAKING THOSE COMMON, EMBARRASSING ERRORS!

### Ron D. Mead, M.A.

Apostrophe? Period? Comma?
Colon? Semicolon? Me or I?
Him or He?
She or Her? Capitalization?
Run-on?
That, Which, or Who?
Comma Splice?

AM
AMETHYST MOON
PUBLISHING

A Concise Grammar Book for Those Who Hate Grammar
© 2010 by Ron D. Mead, M.A.

An Amethyst Moon Book
Published by AMETHYST MOON PUBLISHING
P.O. Box 87885
Tucson, AZ 85754
www.onechoicecanchangealife.com

ISBN-13: 978-1-935354-22-2

ISBN-10: 1-935354-22-1

1st Edition

"I'm amazed at how many people with top education credentials have really poor writing skills. I wonder how they can get credentials and degrees without being able to write sentences that make sense."

--From the National Commission of Writing's Report: *Writing: A Powerful Message from State Governments* (2005)

"States spend nearly a quarter of a billion dollars a year on remedial writing instruction for their employees, according to a new report that says the indirect costs of sloppy writing hurt taxpayers."

--Justin Pope, Associated Press, July 4, 2005

# What College Students and Workshop Participants Say About Ron's Approach to Grammar:[1]

"I liked how I was taught to overcome common errors when writing."

"I have learned the basics in a different and easy way."

"I feel I can take what I learned back to work and produce quality work as well assist my staff members on any writing they produce."

"I liked how quickly I learned."

"I was able to gain an understanding of the common writing errors."

"Now I have more confidence to go back to my job and write business letters, memos, and newsletters."

"I received valuable information to assist me in school and in the workplace."

"Learning quickly helped me to retain the information."

"The information was very useful. It will help me tremendously as I continue my degree as well as in my day-by-day business writing."

"The class helped me dramatically to improve my writing."

"Thank you, Mr. Mead. You have helped me to be more confident with my writing."

"The class took away my writing anxiety because it was easy to follow."

"The class helped me recollect the basic fundamentals of grammar."

"For once I actually feel I learned something I can use."

"I learned a lot that I didn't want to listen to in high school. I enjoyed being in class."

---

[1] These comments are from anonymous course evaluations.

# Appreciation

I wish to thank my loving family members who encouraged me to write this book: Jane, Ted, Rachel, Melody, Dustin, Chris, Rosemary, Craig, and Jody.

I also want to thank my team members for their patience, enthusiasm, and wisdom: Lin Conklin, my publisher; Bret Niemeyer, my mentor; Allan Belleau, my coach; and Lucy, my cattle dog, who nips me at my heals.

# Contents

# The High Cost of Bad Grammar

"Bad writing has recently cost a lawyer—and her firm—more than $6.6 million dollars. A Philadelphia court has ruled that a lease agreement drafted by the lawyer was so 'in artfully [*sic*] written' and 'confusing' that it constituted malpractice."
--From www.manageyourwriting.com (01 June 2007)

"Computer manufacturer Coleco lost $35 million in a single quarter in 1983—and eventually went out of business—when customers purchased its new Adam line of computers, found the instruction manuals unreadable, and rushed to return their computers."
--From www.brunerbiz.com

"An oil company spent hundreds of thousands of dollars developing a new pesticide, only to discover the formula had already been worked out five years earlier by one of the same company's technicians. He wrote his report so poorly that no one had finished reading it."
--From www.brunerbiz.com

"A nuclear plant supervisor ordered 'ten foot long lengths' of radioactive material. Instead of getting the ten-foot long lengths it needed, the plant received ten one-foot lengths, at a cost so great it was later classified."
--From www.brunerbiz.com

# The Shocking Use of Bad Grammar
# in Today's Workplace

Organizations complain that their employees lack good grammar and writing skills. The following postings found on the Internet confirm their complaints:

"Eighty percent of 443 employers surveyed said their workers needed training in writing skills." (Olsten Corp, a placement agency)

"Seventy-five percent of professors and 73% of employers say that the inability of students/employees to write clearly is a major problem." (A Public Agenda – Reality Check survey)

"Writing skills ... of executives are shockingly low, indicating that schools and colleges dismally fail with at least two-thirds of the people who pass through the education pipeline coming out unable to write a simple letter." (Summary of a study published in *Personnel Update*)

"Seventy-nine percent of surveyed executives cited writing as one of the most neglected skills in the business world, yet one of the most important to productivity." (Lin Grensing, communications and HR management expert)

"... Executives identified writing as the most valued skill but said 80 percent of their employees at all levels need to improve." (From a survey of 402 companies reported by the Associated Press)

"The need for workers with writing skills will only increase. Most future jobs will require writing skills." (U.S. Labor Department)

Here are some disturbing comments from the National Commission of Writing's Report, *Writing: A Powerful Message from State Governments* (2005), which includes a survey of state government employees who comment on the bad grammar and poor quality of writing in their offices:

"It appears that providing writing training costs state government about a quarter of a billion dollars annually."

"Grammar is typically the place where applicants fall down. I can't say for sure what proportion, but it's a high enough percentage to get attention."

"Writing today seems like it's getting weaker. That's especially true among applicants for clerical or support positions. We need them all to be able to write. It's very disappointing."

"We are seeing more and more people with very poor skills among new employees. They're not ready to work at the level we need."

"The use of e-mail has had a negative effect on writing clarity. For some, it's just a higher order of instant messaging. Punctuation has disappeared. Nobody uses a period."

"There's no capitalization anymore. It's more like a stream of consciousness and often hard to follow."

# Here is Your Chance to Gain the Competitive Edge!

The workplace *needs* good writers:

"A survey of 120 major American corporations [that employ] nearly eight million people concludes that in today's workplace, writing is a 'threshold skill' for hiring and promotion among salaried (i.e., professional) employees."

"Survey results indicate that writing is a ticket to professional opportunity, while poorly written job applications are a figurative kiss of death. Estimates based on the survey returns reveal that employers spend billions annually correcting writing deficiencies."

From the National Commission of Writing's Report: *Writing: A Powerful Message from State Governments* (2005)

# Why I Wrote This Book in Desperation

This is the heart of the matter: Far too many of *entering* and *graduating* college students write at the middle school level or below. They write incomprehensible sentences, fragments, misspelled words, and incorrect word choice. Some do not know the difference between "their, "they're," and "there" or among "too," "to," and "two."

Here are some examples taken from my students' assignments:

"When a *person* is pushed, *they* (See Rule 10A) may refuse to work with you."

"The elevator bells are used to show *its* (See Rule 11A) average day in hotel lobby (See Rule 8A)."

"Particular Settings (See Rule 15A) that captures (See Rule 9) the *audience* (See Rule 14A) attention (See Rule 8A)."

"He *risk* (See Rule 9) his whole life as he *new* (misspelled) it and attitude change (See Rule 16) and he *looses* (See "Commonly Misused Words") everything (See 8A)."

As you can see, I have had a huge challenge: My students have to learn the basics before they can write college level essays and research papers. This situation presented me with a huge teaching curve that kept me on my toes all the time. I discovered that when *I* corrected their errors, their writing did not improve.

So how did I help these adult learners who were frustrated by their lack of writing skills?

In desperation, I began documenting their grammar errors. After several months, I discovered—to my surprise—that most of my classroom students and my online students were making the same errors. It seemed as if they all had the same English teacher! However, the good news is that students were not making every possible grammar mistake.

I then placed their common errors in what I called "A Quick Guide to Improving Your Writing." I coded (numbered) each rule and gave an example of each error (NO) and how to correct it (YES).

I explained each grammar rule as concisely and clearly as possible, so that I could reference each error in their papers using the word processing's "comments bubble." In this way, they—not me— corrected their own errors.

For example, say a student makes the following error:

"We shall overcome".

Then, I use word processing's "insert comment" utility to point out his or her error. For example, using the error above, I would insert the following comment:

"We shall overcome".

Ron Mead 6/30/10 9:25 PM
Comment: See 13A

Next, the student refers to Rule 13A (shown on the next page), sees the error under NO, and sees how to correct it under YES.

## 13. Correct Use of Quotation Marks, Underlining, and Italics

A. The *comma* and the *period* <u>always</u> go <u>inside</u> quotation marks.

**NO**: One of Hamlet's most famous lines is "To be or not to be".

**YES**: One of Hamlet's most famous lines is "To be or not to be."

As a result, I began to see dramatic improvements in their writing!

I was so excited about this system of helping my students that I could not help but want to share it with teachers, writers, editors, and others.

Moreover, in this book, I have expanded the range of grammar errors to include common "speech grammar" errors that my students make in their discussions and oral presentations. I have also included errors made by public speakers, journalists, advertisers, and television and radio personalities.

As you can see by the comments on pages 11-13, good grammar IS important, and always will be.

I sincerely hope that this book will help you improve your grammar. In turn, perhaps you can help others improve their grammar as well.

Sincerely,

*Ron*

# What Makes This Book Different From Other Grammar Books?

The following are what makes this book different from other grammar books:

1. I have included only the "most common errors" that writers make. I have found that—in most cases—writers can improve their writing quickly by correcting these errors.

2. Unlike many grammar books that have difficult to read, crowded text, I include plenty of white space, so that you can see and grasp the rules and examples quickly.

3. You can also find what you need quickly from the table of contents without the need to refer to a large index.

4. Although some grammatical terms are necessary, I try to refrain from unnecessary grammatical terms. To increase your understanding of the terms used, I have included a "Glossary of Grammatical Terms" that are used in the book.

5. The rules are explained as concisely and clearly as possible.

Although there is some overlap, this book focuses on common grammatical errors, not on effective writing styles.

If writers cannot find what they need in this book, they can refer to the more inclusive grammar books that I have listed in the Resources page.

# How Students, Authors, Journalists, and Other Writers Can Gain the Most From This Book

Refer to the book *while* you are writing.

For example, if you are not sure that you are using a comma correctly, you can refer to "1. Correct Use of Commas." You can do this without wading through pages of a complex grammar book.

Refer to the book *after* you have written something.

If you are not sure that you have written something correctly, check out the rule. This book is a good tool for proofreading your work.

Study one section at time until you have internalized the rules.

For example, first review or memorize "1. Correct Use of Commas." Next, memorize "2. Correct Use of the Semicolon," and so on. Before you know it, you've mastered the rules and can put them into practice!

# How Teachers, Editors, and Reviewers Can Gain the Most From This Book

As a teacher, editor, or reviewer, you can annotate your writers' papers with the codes (numbers). In this way, your writers can correct their own errors and learn to improve their writing in the process.

For example, if your writer uses the semicolon incorrectly, you can use "insert comment" with this coded (numbered) rule: See Rule # 2A. For example:

Edison invented the storage battery; after many failures.

> **Ron Mead 7/7/10 3:47 PM**
> Comment: See #2A

Then your writer can refer to the book, read the concise explanation of how to use the semicolon correctly, see an example of the error under "NO," and learn how to correct it under "YES:"

## 2. Correct Use of the Semicolon (;)

A. Use a *semicolon* (;) to join *two closely related complete sentences* that share a central idea (independent clauses). It *cannot* join sentence fragments (incomplete sentences).

NO: The skyscraper is huge; contains over 500 offices.
--------sentence--------- ----------fragment---------

YES: The skyscraper is huge; it contains cover 500 offices.
---------sentence--------- ------------sentence------------

**Note**: Editors, reviewers, and teachers can also refer to these codes in emails. For example, "To improve your writing, study rules 2A, 12C, and 17C in the book."

# Part I: Grammar Rules

# 1. Correct Use of Commas (,)

The *primary purpose* of the comma is to indicate to your reader when a sentence calls for a brief pause. It also prevents confusion such as "When shooting mother holds her breath" versus "When shooting, mother holds her breath" or "Excited Jane accepted the award" versus "Excited, Jane accepted the award."

**A. Use *one* comma after introductory words, phrases, and clauses.**

**NOTE**: It is correct to use a comma after ALL introductory elements, but they are **required** after each of the following:

**(1)** After **transitional expressions** (*therefore, however, for example, consequently, also*):

He was unpopular. **Consequently**, he did not win the election.

**(2)** After **independent comments** which express the writer's attitude (*obviously, of course, in my opinion*):

**In my opinion**, he should have resigned.

**(3)** After **introductory words, phrases,** and **clauses** that begin a sentence and are placed before the subject and verb of sentence:

**Yes**, we decided he was innocent.
(Introductory word)

**After considering the proposal**, we declined it.
(Introductory phrase)

**After we considered the proposal**, we declined it.
(Introductory clause)

**(4) Do not** use a comma after words and **short** phrases that answer:

**HOW OFTEN**: often, occasionally, frequently
**Occasionally** it happens this way.

**WHERE**: at the conference, in this case
**At the conference** we were given packets.

**WHY**: for this reason, in this case
**In this case** the evidence was against her.

**WHEN**: in nine years, recently, in 2010, yesterday, in the evening
**In 2009** there were several drug arrests.

## B. Use commas with *nonessential* words, phrases, and clauses.

Use **two** commas (one before and one after) internal **nonessential** words, phrases, and clauses that provide additional detail which **can be omitted** without changing the meaning of the sentence. *Internal* nonessential words, phrases, and clauses are those that occur within sentences.

**(1)** With **words**:

NO:  Gracie, however refused the offer.

YES:  Gracie, however, refused the offer.

**(2)** With **phrases**:

NO:  David James on the other hand accepted the offer.

YES:  David James, on the other hand, accepted the offer.

**(3)** With **clauses**:

NO: The engineer who is from Tucson works for us.

YES: The engineer, who is from Tucson, works for us.
(Makes sense without "who is from Tucson.")

**C. Do not use commas with *essential* words, phrases, and clauses that are *necessary* to the meaning of the sentence.**

**(1) Do not** use commas after **initial** *essential* **words**:

NO: **However,** one thinks does not matter.

YES: **However** one thinks does not matter.
("However" is essential to the meaning of the sentence.)

**(2) Do not** use commas **before** and **after** *essential* **phrases**:

NO: The search, **for a cure for cancer,** is still going on.

YES: The search **for a cure for cancer** is still going on.
----essential phrase---

**(3) Do not** use commas **before** and **after** *essential* **clauses**:

NO: The man, **who was to be honored,** was called on stage.

YES: The man **who was to be honored** was called on stage.
-----essential clause------

**(4) Do not** use commas before concluding *essential* **clauses:**

**NO:** Please be on time, **because you are the first speaker.**

**YES:** Please be on time **because you are the first speaker.**
           -----------essential clause------------


**D. Use a comma** *before* **(not after) coordinating conjunctions** (*for, and, nor, but, or, yet, so*[1]) **when they join** *two complete* **sentences:**

**NO:** Frank wanted to go to France **but,** he could not.

**NO:** Frank wanted to go to France, **but** could not.
                              (fragment)

**YES:** Frank wanted to go France, **but** he could not.
       (complete sentence)    (complete sentence)


**E. Use a comma before the final** *and / or* **when joining a** *series* **of** *three* **or** *more* **words and phrases.**

**NO:** Maria enjoys hiking, biking and skiing.

**YES:** Maria enjoys hiking, biking, and skiing.
        --------three words---------

**YES:** Maria enjoys hiking in the desert, biking on trails, and skiing in Utah.
(The three phrases are "hiking in the desert," "biking on trails," and "skiing in Utah.")

---

[1]You can remember these as the FANBOYS (*for, and, nor, but, or, yet, so*).

**F. Do not use a comma before** *and / or* **when they join only** *two* **words and phrases.**

    NO:  I enjoy *cookies*, **and** *milk.*

    YES:  I enjoy *cookies* **and** *milk.*
                -only two words-

    NO:  I like *hiking in the mountains*, **and** *jogging in the desert.*

    YES:  I like *hiking in the mountains* **and** *jogging in the desert.*
            -------------only two phrases-------------------------

**G. Use a comma after** *direct quotations* **preceded by such expressions as** "he said," "she said," "by saying," **and** "replied" **when used with quoted statements, questions, or exclamations.**

    NO:  Martin Luther King **said** "We shall overcome."

    YES:  Martin Luther King **said,** "We shall overcome."

**H. Use commas to set off all** *cities and states, items in dates, addresses* **(except the street number and name), and titles with names.**

Ashtabula, Ohio, is located on Lake Erie.

President Obama lives at 1600 Pennsylvania Avenue, Washington, D. C.

Frank Mario, MD, will be the keynote speaker.

July 4, 1776, was an important day for America.

When using just the month and the year, no comma is necessary after the month or year:

The average snowfall in December 1952 was the highest on record for that month.


**I. Avoid these common comma errors:**


**(1) Comma splice error (fault).** A comma *cannot* join two sentences:

    **NO**: I bake delicious cakes, I have won prizes.
    -------sentence--------- ----sentence-------

To correct a comma splice error (fault), use one of the following: (a) **period** (b) **semicolon** (;) (c) **coordinating conjunction** (*for, and, nor, but, or, yet, so*), or a (d) **conjunctive adverb** (*; therefore, / ; consequently, / ; however,*).

    **(a)** Correct it with a **period**:

    **YES**: I like baking creative cakes. I have won prizes.


    **(b)** Correct it with a **semicolon**:

    **YES**: I like baking delicious cakes; I have won prizes.


    **(c)** Correct it with a **coordinating conjunction**:

    **YES**: I bake delicious cakes, **and** I have won prizes.


    **(d)** Correct it with a **conjunctive adverb**:

    **YES**: I bake delicious cakes; **in fact,** I have won prizes.

**(2) Do not** use commas to separate a verb from its subject unless a modifier comes in between them.

NO: **Graduating** from college**,** **is** his goal.
    subject                  verb

NO: **Graduating** from college **is,** his goal.
    subject                  verb

YES: **Graduating** from college **is** his goal.
    subject                 verb

YES: Dad**,** who is 70 years old**,** just graduated from college.
    subject  -------modifier------     ---verb---


**(3) Do not** insert needless commas (pauses). They interrupt the flow of sentences.

When driving a car, you would not slow down or stop without a reason, would you? So why make your reader pause needlessly? Needless commas interrupt the flow of sentences.

NO: Although**,** he went to class, he did not pay attention.

YES: Although he went to class**,** he did not pay attention.


**(4) Do not** use *ellipsis mark*s ( ... ) as a form of punctuation. (They indicate omissions from quotations.)

NO: The sky was blue ... and then suddenly it rained.

YES: The sky was blue, and then suddenly it rained.

# 2. Correct Use of the Semicolon (;)

**A.** Use a *semicolon* (;) to join *two closely related complete sentences* that share a central idea (independent clauses). It *cannot* join sentence fragments (incomplete sentences).

> **NO:** The skyscraper is huge; contains over 500 offices.
> --------sentence---------   ----------fragment--------

> **YES:** The skyscraper is huge; it contains cover 500 offices.
> ---------sentence--------- ------------sentence------------

**B.** Use a *semicolon* (;) to join *two complete sentences* (independent clauses) when they are linked by a *conjunctive adverb* (*however, consequently, furthermore, otherwise, therefore, then*).

Insert a comma after conjunctive adverbs of **two or more** syllables (*therefore, however, furthermore*) but **no** commas after conjunctive adverbs that contain only one syllable (*then, thus, still*).

> **NO:** The skyscraper is huge**, however**, it contains only 150 offices.

> **YES:** The skyscraper is huge**; however**, it contains only 150 offices.

> **YES:** We took the elevator to the top of the skyscraper**; then** we ate dinner at the Skyview restaurant

**C. To avoid confusion, use a *semicolon* (;) to separate items in a series of the items that *already* contain commas.**

NO: Our company will be represented at the conference by David Jacobus, public affairs officer, Jose Marina, director of personnel, and Maria Conte, safety officer.

YES: Our company will be represented at the conference by David Jacobus, public affairs officer; Jose Marina, director of personnel; and Maria Conte, safety officer.

# 3. Correct Use of the Colon (:)

A. Use a colon—*not a comma or a semicolon*—between two complete sentences when the second sentence *explains* or *illustrates* the first sentence.

A complete sentence *after* the colon may begin with a capital or a small letter, but be consistent.

> **NO:** The term "ethics" has a straightforward definition, it is the study of right and wrong behavior.

> **NO:** The term "ethics" has a straightforward definition; it is the study of right and wrong behavior.

> **YES:** The term "ethics" has a straightforward definition: it is the study of right and wrong behavior.

B. Use a colon to introduce a *series* of words and phrases.

> **YES:** The staff will bring the following items to the meeting: calendars, project plans, and updates.

**C. *Do not* use a colon after the preposition *of* and after verb forms such as *is*, *are*, and *includes* when they are used *within* sentences.**

NO: My favorite novels consist **of:** *Women in Love*, *War and Peace*, and *Pride and Prejudice*.

YES: My favorite novels consist of *Women in Love*, *War and Peace*, and *Pride and Prejudice*.

NO: My favorite novels **are:** *Women in Love*, *War and Peace*, and *Pride and Prejudice*.

YES: My favorite novels are *Women in Love*, *War and Peace*, and *Pride and Prejudice*.

NO: My favorite novels **include:** *Women in Love*, *War and Peace*, and *Pride and Prejudice*.

YES: My favorite novels include the following: *Women in Love*, *War and Peace*, and *Pride and Prejudice*.

YES: My favorite novels are as follows: *Women in Love*, *War and Peace*, and *Pride and Prejudice*.


**D. A colon may be used after *of, is, are*, and *includes* when the items are *listed on separate lines*:**

The team consists of:          The package includes:

    Alex                                15 textbooks
    Naomi                             15 compact discs

# 4. Correct Use of the Hyphen (-)

**A. Use a hyphen[2] to form *compound* (two or more) fractions and numbers.**

    **YES:** two-thirds, thirty-one, thirty-first

**B. Use a hyphen to connect the prefixes *all-, self-, great-*, and *ex-***

    **YES:** all-star, great-grandfather, self-esteem, ex-wife

**C. Use a hyphen to join compound (two or more) adjectives when they come *before* a noun.**

    **YES:** This is a well-written **book**.
                              (noun)

**D. *Do not* use a hyphen to join *compound* (two or more) words when they come *after* a noun or pronoun.**

    **YES:** This is **book** is well written.
                          (noun)

---

[2]Please note the different width of the hyphen as compared to the en and em dashes (See "5. Correct Use of the *em* Dash (—) and the *en* Dash (–).")

# 5. Correct Use of the *em* Dash (—) and the *en* Dash (–)

**A. Use the em dash[3] (—) for *emphasis*:**

> **YES**:  Bonnie—a very smart person—graduated with honors.
> -----emphasizes-----

**B. Use an em dash around *appositives* that contain commas:**

> **YES**:  Bonnie—a very smart, modest person—graduated with honors.

**C. Use the em dash to mark a *dramatic change* in direction:**

> **YES**:  Bonnie is very smart, clever, creative—and a criminal.

**D. Use the en dash[3] (–) to show numerical ranges:**

> **YES**: Read pages 11–22 in your textbook.

---

[3] Please note the different width of the *em* dash and *en* dash as compared with the hyphen (See "4. Correct Use of the Hyphen (-)"). The *em* dash is approximately the size of the letter "m."

# 6. Correct Use of Parentheses ( )

**A.** Use parentheses to contain interesting, helpful but *nonessential* explanations, examples, facts, and comments.

> **YES**: The population of Tucson (now about one million) is still growing.

**B.** When a parenthetical statement is part of a sentence, *do not* place punctuation *before* the opening parenthesis and *do* place the period *outside* the closing parenthesis.

> **NO**: The population of Tucson is growing, (now about one million.)

> **YES**: The population of Tucson is growing (now about one million).

**C.** When a parenthetical statement is placed *after* a complete sentence, capitalize the first word and place the period *inside* the closing parenthesis.

> **YES**: The population of Tucson is growing. (It now has over one million people.)

# 7. Correct Use of Brackets [ ]

**A. Use brackets to include your explanatory words or phrases within a quotation.**

> **YES:** "He [Drew] indicated his displeasure with the outcome."

> **YES:** "Gracie is *suspected* of committing the crime [italics added]."

**B. Use brackets when you change the capitalization of a word within a quotation.**

> **YES:** "… [H]e came to America for a better life."

**C. Use brackets to enclose *"sic"* to show that misspelled words or inappropriately used words are not your own mistakes or words but are part of the quotation:**

> **YES:** "I believe the reportor [*sic*] misquoted me."
> ("reportor" is misspelled.)

# 8. Correct Use of Sentence Structure

**A. Do not write *sentence fragments*. They are incomplete thoughts and do not make sense by themselves.**

**TIP:** Professional writers often read each of their sentences *aloud*—out of context—to check to see if each one makes complete sense. Ask yourself, "Would I say this sentence to someone?"

 **NO:** Be careful of meat. Because it might contain ecoli.
 -------sentence fragment--------

 **YES:** Be careful of meat because it might contain ecoli.

 **YES:** Be careful of meat; it might contain ecoli.

 **YES:** Be careful of meat. It might contain ecoli.

**B. *Do not* write fused (run-on) sentences.**

A *fused* or *run-on* sentence occurs when words "collide" or become "fused" because there is no punctuation (pause) between the sentences.

 **NO:** The ship was **huge its** mast stood 80 feet high.

 ("huge" and "its" run together and are fused)

To correct the error, use one of the following: (a) **period**; (b) **semicolon**; (c) **coordinating conjunction**, or (d) **conjunctive adverb**.

**(a)** Correct it with a **period**:

> **YES:** The ship was huge. Its mast stood 80 feet high.

**(b)** Correct it with a **semicolon**:

> **YES:** The ship was huge; its mast stood 80 feet high.

**(c)** Correct it with a **coordinating conjunction** (*for, and, but, or, yet, so*):

> **YES:** The ship was huge, **and** its mast stood 80 feet high.

**(d)** Correct it with a **conjunctive adverb** (*in addition, for example, moreover*):

> **YES:** The ship was huge; **moreover,** its mast stood 80 feet high.

**C. Do not write** *dangling modifiers*.

When sentences begin with **dangling modifiers** (words, phrases, and clauses), the modifier does not logically agree with the subject of the sentence.

> **NO:** After going home to Ohio, **it** was decided not to stay long.
> ("it" did not decide to stay long!)

To avoid **dangling modifiers**, be sure that your introductory modifier logically modifies the subject of the sentence which follows it.

> **YES**: After going home to Ohio, **Craig** decided not to stay long.
> ("Craig" decided not to stay long)

## D. Do not write *misplaced modifiers*.

These are words or phrases that are "misplaced" and modify the wrong words.

> **NO**: If you want to, you can meet with our consultant with work issues.
> (The consultant does not have work issues!)

To avoid **misplaced modifiers**, be sure to place modifying words and phrases logically *near* the words they modify.

> **YES**: If you have work issues, you can meet with our consultant.

## E. Do not write *squinting modifiers*.

These modifiers make you "squint" because they are placed in such a way that can be interpreted as modifying either what precedes them or what follows them.

> **NO**: Missing work frequently can hurt an employee's work record.
>
> (Is it "frequently missing work" or "frequently can hurt an employee's work record"?)

> **YES**: Frequently missing work can hurt an employee's work record.

> **YES**: An employee's work record can be hurt by his or her missing work frequently.

**F. Do not write** *split infinitives*.

Infinitives are formed by *to* + *verb* (to eat, to work, to sleep).
Do not insert a word between "to" and the verb.

**NO**: Lin began *to* **cautiously** *enter* the lion's cage.

**YES**: Lin **cautiously** began *to enter* the lion's cage.

**YES**: Lin began *to enter* the lion's cage **cautiously**.

**YES**: Lin began, **cautiously**, *to enter* the lion's cage.

**YES**: **Cautiously**, Lin began *to enter* the lion's cage.

## G. Do not write sentences that lack *parallel structure*.

To express like ideas in parallel form, adjectives should be *matched* by adjectives, nouns by nouns, phrases by phrases, and clauses by clauses.

These two highlighted words **do not** match in form:

    **NO**:  The new class was **interesting** and a **challenge**.
                      (adjective)       (noun)

These two highlighted words **do** match in form:

    **YES**:  The new class was **interesting** and **challenging**.
                      (adjective)    (adjective)

These two highlighted words **do not** match in form:

    **NO**:  Ted and Rachel enjoy **skiing** and **to hike**.
                    (verbal)   (infinitive)

These two highlighted words **do** match in form:

    **YES**:  Ted and Rachel enjoy **skiing** and **hiking**.
                    (verbal)   (verbal)

# 9. Correct Agreement Between Subjects and Verbs

Make your **subjects** and **verbs** agree in number. <u>Singular</u> verbs end in "s" (goes, disciplines, seeks*).* <u>Plural</u> verbs *do not* end in "s" *(go, discipline, seek).*

**A. If the** *subject* **is <u>singular</u>, then the** *verb* **must be <u>singular</u>.**

> **NO:** An effective *parent* **discipline** their child.
>         (singular) (plural)

> **YES:** An effective *parent* **disciplines** his or her child.
>          (singular) (singular)

**B. If the** *subject* **is <u>plural</u>, then the** *verb* **must be <u>plural</u>.**

> **YES:** Effective *parents* **discipline** their children.
>          (plural)   (plural)

# 10. Correct Agreement Between Pronouns and Antecedents

Make **pronouns** (*he, she, they*) agree in number with their **antecedents** (the word for which the pronoun stands for).

**A. If a *pronoun* is <u>singular</u>, then its *antecedent* must be <u>singular</u>.**

> **NO:**  A **parent** must discipline **their** child.
>     (singular)              (plural)

> **YES:**  A **parent** must discipline **his or her** child.
>     (singular)              (singular)

**B. If a *noun* (subject) is <u>plural</u>, then its *antecedent* must be <u>plural</u>.**

> **NO:**  **Parents** must discipline **his or her** children.
>     (plural)             (singular)

> **YES:**  **Parents** must discipline **their** children.[4]
>     (plural)             (plural)

> **NO:**  If **one** does not want to attend the meeting, **they** must say so.
>     (singular)                      (plural)

> **YES:**  If **one** cannot attend the meeting, **he or she** must say so.
>     (singular)                (singular)

> **YES:** If **employees** cannot attend the meeting, **they** must say so.[4]
>     (plural)                (plural)

---

[4]It is better usage to match plural nouns with plural pronouns than the awkward use of "he or she."

**C. When a pronoun refers to a *collective noun* (General Motors, Department of the Treasury), the pronoun is <u>singular</u>.**

NO:  **General Electric** has **their** policies.
      (singular)       (plural)

YES:  **General Electric** has **its** policies.
      (singular)     (singular)

NO:  **Mathematics are** my favorite subject.
     (singular) (plural)

YES:  **Mathematics is** my favorite subject.
     (singular) (singular)

# 11. Correct Use of Pronoun Reference

**A. Avoid** *ambiguous reference of pronouns.*

This error occurs when your reader does not know exactly what your pronoun refers to. Therefore, you sometimes need to repeat words for clarity.

> **NO**:  Ethel told Lucy that **her** essay was well written.
> (Whose essay was well written, Ethel's or Lucy's?)

> **YES**:  Ethel told Lucy that **Lucy's** essay was well written.

> **NO**: The file folders, alphabetized by the employees, were out of order, so we sent **them** back to headquarters.
> (Sent the employees or the files back to headquarters?)

> **YES**:  The file folders, alphabetized by the employees, were out of order, so we sent the **file folders** back to headquarters.

**B. Avoid** *implied antecedents.*

These are pronouns that do not clearly refer to a noun.

Correct **implied antecedents** by naming the *real* nouns.

> **NO**:  Although the game was over, **it** was not clear which team had won.

> **YES**:  Although the game was over, **Jessica** was not clear which team had won.

**C. Avoid *vague reference of pronouns*.**

This error occurs when you use them to refer to vague, unnamed entities.

Be sure that you do not use pronouns that have no clear reference:

> **NO**: In this book **it** says that Thomas Jefferson's slaves were freed after he died.

> **YES**: In this book **the author** writes that Thomas Jefferson's slaves were freed after Jefferson died.

## 12. Correct Use of Pronoun Case

Pronouns have three cases.

- **Subjective case** pronouns (*I, we, he, she, it,* and *they*) are used as subjects of verbs and with forms of "to be."

- **Objective case** pronouns (*me, us, him, her, or them*) are used as objects of verbs or prepositions.

- **Possessive case** pronouns express ownership.


**A. Use the *subjective case* pronouns when they used as *subjects* of verbs.**

> **NO**: (*Me, us, him, her, or them*) **threw** the ball.

> **YES**: (*I, we, he, she, it, or they*) **threw** the ball.

**TIP**: In compound sentences, where there are two pronouns or a noun and a pronoun joined by **and**, remove the "and" and read each subject and verb separately. Then, you can see which pronoun case you will need.

> **NO**: Bret **and** me travel a good deal.
> (Remove the "and" to test it: Would you say, "Me travel"?)

> **YES**: Bret **and** I travel a good deal.
> (Remove the "and" to test it: "Bret travels." "I travel.")

> **NO**: Us women like our new leader.
> (Would you say, "Us like our new leader"?)

> **YES**: We women like our new leader.
> (We like our new leader.)

**B.** Use the *subjective case* of pronouns with forms of "to be" (*is, was, were, are)*:

**NO**: It **was** (*me, her, him, us, them*) who called.

**YES**: It **was** (*I, she, he, we, they*) who called.

**NO**: It was **me** who gave the donation.

**YES**: It was **I** who gave the donation.

**NOTE**: Although ungrammatical, people often say, "It's me," "It's her," and "It's him." It seems to be accepted in everyday speech, but it is not in formal writing.

**C.** Use the *subjective case* in comparisons that usually follow with "than" or "as."

These comparisons omit words such as those in the parentheses in the sentences below.

**NO**: He is smarter than me (am).
(Would you say, "He is smarter than **me am** smarter?")

**YES**: He is smarter than I (am).

**NO**: This helps you as much as (it helps) I.

**YES**: This helps you as much as (it helps) me.

**NO**: She is as adventersome as me (am).

**YES**: She is as adventuresome as I (am).

**D.** Use the *objective case* of pronouns as *objects* of verbs and prepositions:

**NO:** Throw (*I, we, he, she, they*) the ball.

**YES:** Throw (*me, us, him, her, them*) the ball.

**NO:** Please throw the ball to (*I, we, he, she, they*).

**YES:** Please throw the ball to (*me, us, him, her, them*)

**NO:** They gave the plants to Jane **and** I.
(To test the above, remove the "and." Would you say, "They gave the plants to *I*"?)

**YES:** They gave the plants to Jane **and** me.
(To test the above, remove the "and." "They gave the plants to Jane." "They gave the plants to *me*.")

**E. Use *who* as the subject of a verb.**

**TIP:** To test for correct usage, substitute *he*, *she*, or *they*.

**NO:** Whom is the CEO of this company?

**YES:** Who **is** the CEO of this company?
(Test it: she or he is the CEO of this company)

**F. Use *whom* in the objective case because it is used as object of prepositions and verbs.**

**TIP:** To test for correct usage, substitute *him, her,* or *them* which are objective case pronouns (See 12D).

**YES:** **Whom** am I talking to (preposition)?
(Test it: Am I talking to *him, her,* or *them*?)

**YES:** **Whom** did you recommend (verb) for the position?
(The test: Did you recommend *him* for the position?)

# 13. Correct Use of Quotation Marks, Underlining, and Italics

**A.** The *comma* and the *period* <u>always</u> go <u>inside</u> quotation marks.

**NO**: One of Hamlet's most famous lines is "To be or not to be".

**YES**: One of Hamlet's most famous lines is "To be or not to be."

**B.** Use *quotation marks*—not underlining or italics—for *minor or shorter* works such as short stories, poems, songs, articles, essays, TV episodes, and book chapters:

**NO**: Juan's favorite song is *Happy Birthday*.
(italics)

**NO**: Juan's favorite song is <u>Happy Birthday</u>.
(underlining)

**YES**: Juan's favorite song is "Happy Birthday."
(quotation marks)

**C.** Use *underlining* or *italics* — not quotation marks — for *major or longer* works such as books, plays, pamphlets, long musical works, TV and radio programs, long poems, periodicals, published speeches, movies, videos, and works of visual art.

**NO:**  Juan's favorite movie is "It's a Wonderful Life."
(quotation marks)

**YES:**  Juan's favorite movie is *It's a Wonderful Life.*
(italics)

**YES:**  Juan's favorite movie is It's a Wonderful Life.
(underlining)

**D.** Use *single* quotation marks (' ') to indicate certain titles and quotations within quotations.

**YES:**  He asked, "Did you know that Billie Holiday sang 'Strange Fruit'?"
(The question mark is placed after the single quotation mark because it refers to the question asked.)

**YES:**  He asked, "How many times did Martin Luther King repeat 'I have a dream' in his famous speech?"

# 14. Correct Use of the Apostrophe (')

**A. Use the *apostrophe* to show *singular* or *plural* possession, not the plural form of nouns.**

**NO**: We go to the **farmers** market on Saturdays.

**YES**: We go to the **farmer's** market on Saturdays.
(One farmer at his or her market.)

**YES**: We go to the **farmers'** market on Saturdays.
(More than one farmer at the market.)

**NO**: We see the **farmer's** at the market.

**YES**: We see the **farmers** at the market.
(plural)

**B. Use *its* and *it's* correctly**

"Its" is possessive.

"It's" is the contraction for "it is."

**NO**: Give the dog **it's** food.
(This says, "Give the dog *it is* food.")

**YES**: Give the dog **its** food.
(possessive)

## C. Do not use the apostrophe when forming the plural forms of dates and abbreviations:

| NO: | YES: |
|-----|------|
| 1970's | 1970s |
| Ph.D's | Ph.Ds |
| CD's | CDs |
| 401(k)'s | 401(k)s |

**Exception**: Use an apostrophe before the "s" with some letters to prevent confusion as in the "three R's."

NO:  He received three **As** in computer science.
(Reads like "as.")

YES:  He received three **A's** in computer science.

## D. Use an apostrophe to show the possessive case of nouns and pronouns *before* gerunds.

A gerund is a form of a verb (verbal) that ends in -*ing* and functions as a noun.

NO:  **Jane running** improved her blood pressure.
(gerund)

YES:  **Jane's running** improved her blood pressure.
(gerund)

NO:  We were impressed with **him** *doing* the job.

YES:  We were impressed with **his** *doing* the job.

## 15. Correct Use of Capitalization

**A.** *Do not* **capitalize** *common nouns* (general terms of classification).

**NO:** Dog, Reader, University, City, Government, President, Department.

**YES:** dog, reader, university, city, government, president, department

**B. Capitalize names of departments, languages, organizations, government agencies, institutions, companies, people, and things.**

Capitalize historical events, holidays, religions, trademarks, days of the week, months, geographical names, acronyms, holy days, religious believers, holy books, historical periods or eras, titles of persons when these come before names, the first words of directly quoted speeches, and major words in the titles of books, plays, essays, movies, and so on.

**NO:** He works in *Sanitation*.

**YES:** He works in *sanitation*.

**YES:** He works in the *Sanitation Department*.
(name of the department)

**C. Capitalize titles *before* a person's name.**

**Do not** capitalize titles when they come *after* or apart from names.

**NO:** Clark, Provost of King's College

**YES:** Clark, provost of King's College

**YES:** Provost Clark of King's College

**YES:** We know the provost of King's College.

**D. Capitalize the first, last, and important words in titles and subtitles of works.**

**Do not** capitalize articles (*a, an, the*), prepositions *of, to, with*, and conjunctions (*for, and, nor, but, or, yet*) **unless** they appear after a colon.

**NO:** *Identifying Birds: what to Look For*

**YES:** *Indentifying Birds: What to Look For*

**YES:** *My Life: A Confession*

## 16. Correct Use of Coordinating Conjunctions (*for, and, nor, but, or, yet, so*)

**Select the correct coordinating conjunction** (*for, and, nor, but, or, yet, so*) **to express the correct meaning:**

- Use *and* to show an addition and sequence.

- Use *but*, *yet*, and *nor* to show exception.

- Use *so* and *for* to show cause and effect or consequence.

**NO:** David wanted to go, **and** he decided not to.

**YES:** David wanted to go, **but** he decided not to.
(exception)

**YES:** Judy washed the dishes **and** kitchen floor.
(addition)

**YES:** Judy washed the dishes **and** then went to bed.
(sequence)

**NO:** Lupe became ill, **and** she did not attend class.

**YES:** Lupe became ill, **so** she did not attend class.
(consequence)

# 17. Correct Use of Numbers

**A.** Spell out (use words) for numbers 1 through 10. Use *numerals* for all numbers over 10.

    **NO:** There are **eleven** students in the class.

    **YES:** There are **11** students in the class.

    **NO:** There are **10** people in the class.

    **YES:** There are **ten** people in the class.

**B.** Spell out (use words) all numbers that can be written in *two words*.

    **NO:** There are **31** days in July.

    **YES:** There are **thirty-one** days in July.

**C.** Use figures when *more than two words* are required.

    **NO:** There are **three hundred and sixty five** days in a year.

    **YES:** There are **365** days in a year.

**D. Spell out numbers that *begin* sentences.**

> **NO:** **1 million** dollars is not much money these days.

> **YES:** **One million** dollars is not much money these days.

**E. Use either all numerals or all words when many numbers are in the same sentence.**

> **NO:** Jessica owns three thousand head of cattle, 400 sheep, and fifty-two hogs.

> **YES:** Jessica owns 3,000 head of cattle, 400 sheep, and 52 hogs.

> **YES:** Jessica owns three thousand head of cattle, four hundred sheep, and fifty-two hogs.

## 18. Correct Use of the Past Tense

Add "-d" or "-ed" to approprite words to form the past tense (events that happened in the past).

NO:  Alan was **suppose** to submit his report by Monday.

YES: Alan was **supposed** to submit his report by Monday.

NO:  She was **use** to being mistreated.

YES: She was **used** to being mistreated.

## 19. Correct Use of Indefinite Articles (*a*, *an*) and the Definite Article (*the*)

**A. Use indefinite articles (*a*, *an*) before nouns that are nonspecific, singular, and countable (individual items that you can count and cannot view as a mass).**

> **YES:** Please give me *a* file folder.
> (Not a specific file folder.)

**B. Use "a" before consonant sounds (*b, c, d, f, g, h, j, k, l, m, n, p, q, r, s, t, v, w, x, y, z*):**

> **YES:** Bonnie had to write *a* medical report.

**C. Use "an" before vowel sounds (*a, e, i, o, u*):**

> **YES:** I had to write *an* annual report.

**D. Use the definite article (*the*) to refer to *specific* nouns.**

> **YES:** Please give me *the* file folder that contains *the* statistics.

## 20. Correct Use of the Subjunctive Mood

Use the *subjunctive mood* to express wishes, orders, and conditions contrary to fact (use *were, be* versus *was, is*).

### A. To express wishes:

NO: Frank wishes he **was** in Dallas for the game.

YES: Frank wishes he **were** in Dallas for the game.

### B. To express orders:

NO: Their requirement is that everyone **is** trained.

YES: Their requirement is that everyone **be** trained.

### C. To express conditions contrary to fact:

NO: If I **was** you, I would not take the job.

YES: If I **were** you, I would not take the job.

## 21. Correct Use of Past Participle and Past Tense Verb Forms

**A. Here are some past participle verb forms:** *gone, done, begun, broken, chosen, come, drunk, eaten, frozen, grown, known, lent, spoken, written. rung,* and *seen.*

These forms must be used with *helping* (auxiliary) verbs such as *be, been, is, was, were, has, have,* and *had.*

**NO:** I **seen** him around campus.

**YES:** I **have seen** him around campus.

**NO:** Jennifer **had chose** not to attend the training class.

**YES:** Jennifer **had chosen** not to attend the training class.

**B. Here are the past tense verb forms of the above past participle forms:** *went, did, began, broke, chose, came, drank, ate, froze, grew, knew, lent, spoke, wrote, rang,* and *saw.*

Unlike the above past participle forms above, the past tense forms **do not** require helping (auxiliary) verb forms.

**NO:** I **had saw** him on campus.

**YES:** I **saw** him on campus.

**YES:** Jennifer **chose** not to attend the training class.

## 22. Correct Use of Negatives in Sentences

Use only *one* negative in a sentence such as *scarcely, barely*, and *hardly*. Do not use the *double negative*.

NO: I **don't** want **none** of the candy.
    (negative)  (negative)

YES: I **don't** want **any** of the candy.
    (negative)  (positive)

NO: I **don't** want to go **nowhere** with her.
    (negative)          (negative)

YES: I **don't** want to go **anywhere** with her.
    (negative)         (positive)

NO: I **couldn't hardly** wait to go to the game.
    (negative)(negative)

YES: I **could hardly** wait to go to the game.
    (positive)(negative)

NO: I **don't** want **nothing** from him.
    (negative)   (negative)

YES: I **don't** want **anything** from him.
    (negative)    (positive)

# Part II:  Commonly Misused Words

## affect, effect

**A.** *Affect* means "to influence."

To test for correct use of *affect*, substitute "influences."

**YES:** Spring *affects* (influences) my allergies.

**B.** *Effect* means result.

**YES:** Many drugs have side *effects* (results).

## all right, alright

Use *all right*; alright is misspelled.

**YES:** If it *all right* with you, we will meet tomorrow.

## a lot, alot

Use *a lot*; alot is misspelled.

**YES:** There are *a lot* of discarded cell phones in landfills.

## among, between

**A.** Use *between* when it involves only *two* people or items.

**YES:** The choice is *between* **two** software programs.

**B.** Use *among* when it refers to *more than* two people or items.

**YES:** The choice is *among* **three** software programs.

## amount

**A.** *Amount* refers to items that are **not** countable.

**YES:** We have a large *amount* of work to do today.
("Work" can not be counted: One work? Two work?)

**B.** *Number* refers to items that **are** countable.

**YES:** I have a large *number* of tasks to complete today.
("Tasks" can be counted: One, two, three tasks.)

## anyways, nowheres

These words are misspelled. Do not use them in formal writing.

**NO:** I am not going *anyways*.

**YES:** I am not going *anyway*.

## as, as if, like

A. Use *as* or *as if*—not **like**—to introduce subordinate (dependent) clauses.

**NO:** The new program worked *like* we hoped it would.

**YES:** The new program worked *as* we hoped it would.
------a full clause-----

**YES:** It seemed *as if* the program might fail.
--------a full clause-----------

B. Use *like* in comparisons.

**YES:** Other programs *like* it have failed.

## as good, as good as, better than

Use *as good as*—not **as good**—for complete comparisons.

**NO:** She is *as good* at sports as he is.

**YES:** She is *as good as* he is at sports.

**YES:** She is *better than* he is at sports.

**at**

Do not end a sentence with the preposition *at*.

**NO:** Where are you *at*?

**YES:** Where are you?

**bad, badly**

A. Use the adjective *bad* to describe how something looks, tastes, and feels.

**YES:** The food tastes *bad*.

B. Use the adverb *badly* to describe how something works or runs.

**YES:** The car runs *badly*.

**between you and I, between you and me**

*Between you and I* is incorrect. *Between you and me* is correct because "me" is objective of the preposition "between."

**YES:** This whole matter is *between you and me* (not "I").
(Would you say "between I"?)

**choose, chose**

    **A.** Use *chose* for the past tense.

    **YES**: Yesterday, I *chose* not to go to the game.

    **B.** Use *choose* to mean "elect."

    **YES**: I *choose* (elect) not to go to the game.

    **C.** Use *choose* to mean making a selection.

    **YES**: I found it hard to *choose* (select) which one I wanted.

**could of, should of, might of**

    Do not use *could of*, *should of*, or *might of*. Replace *of* with *have*:

    **YES**: We *could have*, *should have*, and *might have*.

**couple of, two**

    Use *two*, not "couple of" which is wordy.

    **YES**: The new governing body had *two* (not "a couple of") issues to deal with.

## definately, definitely

"Definately" is misspllelled. Use *definitely*.

**YES**: I will *definitely* be there.


## due to, because of

*Due to* means "caused by." It should be used only if it can be substituted with "caused by." It is used after forms of "to be" (*was, is, were*). It does not mean the same as "because of."

**NO**: The class was cancelled *due to* snow.

**YES**: The class was cancelled *because of* rain.

**YES**: The class's cancellation was *due to* (caused by) rain.


## due to the fact, because or since

Use *because* or *since*, not the wordy expression "due to the fact that."

**NO**: The computer's failure is *due to the fact that* a virus crippled it.

**YES**: The computer failed *because* (or *since*) a virus crippled it.

**every day, everyday**

A. Use *every day* when you can substitute "each day."

YES: The computer system goes down *every day* (each day).

B. Use *everyday* as an adjective to modify or describe words.

YES: The system's going down is an *everyday* occurrence.


**etc.**

Avoid *etc.* Be precise.

NO:   For our meeting, please bring your agenda, *etc.*

YES:   For our meeting, please bring your agenda and calendar.


**farther, further**

A. *Farther* refers to additional distance.

YES: It was much *farther* to town than we thought.

TIP: Remember it by the prefix "far" in "farther."

B. *Further* means additional time or amount.

YES: We will not discuss this issue any *further*.

## fewer, less

A. Use *fewer* with items that "can be counted."

**YES**: There were *fewer* transactions than yesterday.
(Transactions <u>can be</u> counted: One, two, three transactions.)

B. Use *less* with items that "cannot be counted."

**YES**: We had *less* work to complete today.
(Work <u>cannot</u> be counted: One work? Two work?)

## from, form

Although the spell checker recognizes both words as being spelled correctly, they have different meanings.

**NO**: Please sign the *from form* the front office.

**YES**: Please sign the *form from* the front office.

## good, well

A. Use *good* as an adjective to describe something or someone.

**YES:** He a *good* athlete.

B. Use *well* as an adverb to describe "how" things are done.

**NO:** The car runs *good*.

**YES:** The car runs *well*.

C. Use *well* as an adjective to refer to health.

**NO:** He feels *good*.

**YES:** He feels *well*.

## their, there, they're

A. Use *their* to show possession.

**YES:** It is *their* ball game.

B. Use *there* when referring to a place, whether specific or more abstract.

**YES:** It is over *there*.

**YES:** It must be difficult to live *there*.

C. Use *they're* as a contraction meaning "they are."

**YES:** *They're* (they are) coming to our party.

**is when, is where**

A. Do not use *when* after *is*. Use a noun form.

NO:  Totalitarianism *is when* citizens are totally subject to an absolute state authority.

YES:  Totalitarianism *is a concept* (noun) that citizens should be totally subject to an absolute state authority.

*(From merriam-webster.com/dictionary/totalitarianism)*

B. Do not use *where* after *is*. Use a noun form.

NO:  Socialism *is where* a system or condition of society in which the means of production are owned and controlled by the state.

YES:  Socialism *is a system* (noun) or condition of society in which the means of production are owned and controlled by the state.

*(From merriam-webster.com/dictionary/socialism)*

**it's, its**

A. *It's* is a contraction for "it is."

YES:  *It's* (it is) a nice day to walk the dog.

B. *Its* is the possessive form.

YES:  I gave my dog *its* (not "it is") bone.
         (The dog possesses the bone.)

**lay, lie**

A. *Lay*, *laying*, and *laid* mean to "place" and requires direct objects.

   **YES**:  She *laid* the *silverware* out of sight.
            (She laid what? The silverware. The silverware is the direct object of the verb "laid.")

B.  *Lie*, *lying*, and *lain* mean to "recline" and have no direct objects.

   **YES**:  She was *lying* (reclining not "laying") on the sofa.
            (In contrast to "laying," you can not say "lying what?")

**lets, let's**

A. Use "lets" as a verb.

   **YES**:  Maria *lets* her boy swim at the community pool.

B. Use *let's* as the contraction for "let us."

   **YES**:  *Let's* (let us) go to the movies.

**loose, lose**

A.  As a verb, *lose* means "cease to have."

   **YES**:  Did you *lose* your dog?

B.  As an adjective, *loose* means "not tight."

   **YES**:  The dog has a *loose* collar.

**moral, morale**

**A.** *Moral* is an adjective referring to right and wrong behavior.

**YES**: He is a *moral* person.

**B.** *Morale* is a noun that means "spirit."

**YES**: The *morale* (spirit) of the troops is high.

**myself, me**

**A.** Use *me*, not "myself" as a pronoun.

**NO**: The whereabouts of the key was only known to him and *myself*.

**YES**: The whereabouts of the key was only known to him and *me*.

**B.** Use the intensive word *myself* "to intensify" statements.

**YES**: I *myself* did the job.

**C.** Use the reflexive word *myself* to "reflect back" to the subject.

**YES**: I did the job all by *myself*.

**NOTE**: The above rule also applies to the use of *himself, herself, yourself*, and *itself*.

## okay, OK, O.K.

Avoid these abbreviations in formal writing.

**NO:** It is *okay* to enter the building.

**YES:** It is *all right* enter the building.


## plus, in addition

Do not use *plus* as a coordinating conjunction or as a transitional expression. Use *plus* to mean "in addition to."

**NO:** *Plus*, the company went into bankruptcy.

**YES:** *In addition*, the company went into bankruptcy.

**YES:** Judy's stocks *plus* ("in addition to") her assets made her wealthy.


## quite, quiet

A. *Quiet* means "not loud."

**YES:** She is a *quiet* person.

B. *Quite* means "to a considerable extent."

**YES:** Therefore, it was *quite* a gesture on her part not to speak out.

## quote, quotation

*Quote* is a verb; *quotation* is a noun.

**YES**: He added *quotations* (not *quotes*) to his paper.

**YES**: May I *quote* you?


## reason is because, reason is that

Do not use *the reason is because*. It is redundant. Use *the reason is that* or *because* by itself.

**NO**: The *reason* the computer failed *is because* it contained a virus.

**YES**: The *reason* the computer failed *is that* it contained a virus.

**YES**: The computer failed *because* it contained a virus.


## than, then

**A.** *Than* is used for comparison.

**YES**: My dog is larger *than* your dog.

**B.** *Then* indicates time.

**YES**: I saw him *then*.

**that, who, which**

A. Use *that* when referring to a type or class of person.

**YES:** He is the kind of person *that* (not "who") would fit in anywhere.

B. Use *who* when referring to individuals.

**YES:** Lance is a Boy Scout *who* (not "that") loves camping.

C. Use *which* and *that* when referring to items, animals, and places.

**YES:** The movie, *which* (or "that") was praised by critics, won an award.

**these ones, those ones**

**NO:** *These ones* are yours.

**YES:** *These items* are yours.

**NO:** *Those ones* are yours.

**YES:** *Those items* are yours.

**through, thru**

Use *through*, not "thru" (misspelled).

**YES**: Hc was *through* (not thru) with the book.


**too, to, two**

**A**. *Too* is an adverb that means "also" or "excessively."

**YES**: Many snowbirds leave Tucson when it gets *too* (not "to") hot.

**B**. *To* is a preposition.

**YES**: The snowbirds left Tucson *to* (not "too") return *to* (not "too") Minnesota.

**C**. *Two* is the word for the number two.

**YES**: *Two* of my friends came to dinner.


**try and, try to**

Use *try to*, not "try and."

**YES**: I will *try to* (not "try and") be on time.

**unique, most unique**

*Unique* means "the only one of its kind," so do not use *very* and *most* with it.

**NO**: Some say the café is *very unique*, and others say it is the *most unique* café in town.

**YES**: Some say that the café is *unique*.


**youse guyses, you guys**

*Youse guyses* is misspelled. *Youse guyses* and *you guys* are slang terms. Do not use either in formal writing.

**NO**: I'll meet *youse guyses* at the game.

**YES**: I'll meet *you guys* at the game.
       (informal use)


**you know, like, I mean, whatnot, and stuff like that**

Avoid these empty *fillers* which say nothing and are distracting.

**NO**: The movie, *I mean*, had *like* some good action scenes in it and *stuff like that, you know*.

**YES**: The movie had some good action scenes in it.

## who's, whose

**A.** *Who's* is a contraction for "who is."

**NO:** *Whose* coming to our meeting?

**YES:** *Who's* coming to our meeting?

**B.** *Whose* is the possessive form of "who."

**YES:** *Whose* (not "who's") car is this?

**YES:** Do you know *whose* (not "who's") pen this is?

**YES:** I know a woman *whose* (not "who's") parents live in Alaska.

**YES:** *Whose* (not "who's") side are you on?

## would be, is

When appropriate, use *is* rather than "would be." In the following example, "would be" is a weak verb form.

**NO:** A good example *would be* how the character uses language.

**YES:** A good example *is* how the character uses language.

# Part III: Glossary of Grammatical Terms

The following terms are explained briefly to help you gain a better understanding of the rules. To improve your grammar, however, you will need to refer to the rules to see the grammar errors and how to correct them.

**Adjective**—a word used to describe or limit the meaning of a noun.

He owns a *large* house.

**Adverb**—a word used to describe a verb, adjective, or another adverb.

He hit the ball *far*. (Describes the *verb* "hit.")

He is an *exceptionally* good ball player. (Describes the *adjective* "good.")

He hit the ball *very* far. (Describes the *adverb* "far")

**Antecedent**—the noun for which a pronoun stands for.

*George Washington* (antecedent) lived at Mount Vernon, Virginia; *he* (pronoun) also had a home in Alexandria, Virginia.

**Appositive**—a noun or noun phrase that renames another noun right next to it.

The classic *car*, a *Duesenberg*, won first price at the car show.

**Apostrophe** has three uses:

1. To form possessives of nouns:

   *Clark's* Furniture Outlet

2. To show the omission of letters in contractions:

   He *couldn't* attend the conference.

3. To indicate certain plurals of lowercase letters:

   Jessica earned straight *A's* (not As) in college.

**Brackets [ ]** are used to include your explanatory words or phrases within quotations.

"Columbus [Ohio] has a lot to offer a visitor."

**Colon (:)**—Among other uses, it is used before a list.

Please order the following items: pens, paper, and ink.

**Collective nouns** are words used to define a *group* of objects, where objects can be people, animals, emotions, inanimate things, concepts, or other things. They require singular verbs.

General Motors *is* (not "are") an automotive company.

**Comma**—The purpose of the comma is to make sentences easier to understand by creating pauses between elements that need to be separated.

When shooting my mother holds her breath.

(Shooting my mother?

When shooting, my mother holds her breath.

**Comma splice error (fault)**—A comma cannot join two sentences.

Rachel runs races, she is a fast runner.
-----sentence------ ------sentence------

**Conjunctive adverb**—an *adverb* that connects ("conjuncts") two sentences. They show cause and effect, sequence, contrast, comparison, or other relationships. Examples: *however, therefore, nevertheless, then, too, also, furthermore, moreover, indeed, still, thus, otherwise, consequently, accordingly,* and *more*.

Chris composes classical music; *furthermore,* he plays his own compositions.

**Coordinating conjunctions** join two sentences of equal importance. *For, and, nor, but, or, yet* and *so* are the coordinating conjunctions. (They can be remembered by the acronym "FANBOYS.")

**Dangling modifiers** and **misplaced modifiers** are words, phrases, or clauses that do not clearly modify what they are meant to modify.

**Definite article**—the word *the*.

**Dependent (subordinate) clause**—a part of a sentence that contains a subject and verb. It is not a complete sentence on its own. It "depends" upon an independent clause (sentence) to make sense.

> Although he behaved well, he was he was not granted parole.
> (Dependent clause)        (Independent clause/sentence)

**Direct quotation**—a report of the exact words expressed orally or verbally by others. (Compare with "indirect quotation.")

> Martin Luther King said, "I have a dream."

**Ellipsis marks** ( ... )—indicate an intentional omission of word(s) in a quotation.

Original quotation:

> "The ceremony honored twelve brilliant athletes from the Caribbean who were visiting the U.S."

With "from the Caribbean omitted":

> "The ceremony honored twelve brilliant athletes ... who were visiting the U.S."

**Em Dash** (—) Among other uses, it is used to create emphasis. The dash is also known as an "em dash" because it is the length of a printed letter "m" and is longer than a hyphen or an "en dash."

**Essential words, phrases, and clauses**—these provide *essential* information which *can not* be omitted without changing the meaning of the sentence. No commas are used before and after them.

> The search *for a cure for Alzheimer's Disease* is still going on.
> ---------------essential----------------

**Gerund** is a verb form (verbal) that ends in *-ing* and functions as a noun. When a noun comes before a gerund, add 's to the noun. When a pronoun comes before a gerund, the pronoun must be in the possessive case.

> They objected to the youngest *girl's* (not "girl") being given the command position.

**Hyphen** (-)—It is used between parts of a compound word or name. It is also used to split a word by syllables to fit on a line of text.

> The *seventy-year-old* man is a *full-time* college student.

**Indefinite articles**—the words *a* and *an*.

**Independent clause**—a complete sentence that contains a subject and verb and makes sense by itself.

> Although he behaved well, he was not granted parole.
> (Dependent clause)    (Independent clause/sentence)

**Indirect quotation**—a paraphrase of someone else's words. It is placed in quotation marks. (Compare with the direct quotation, above.)

> Martin Luther King repeated the words "I have a dream" in his famous speech.

**Intensive pronoun**—a word used to *intensify* (emphasize) a noun or pronoun, with the suffix *-self*. When it is removed, the sentence still makes sense. (Compare with "reflexive pronoun.")

> The CEO *himself* called the meeting.

**Nonessential words, phrases, and clauses**—these provide additional descriptive or explanatory detail which can be omitted *without* changing the meaning of the sentence. These require a comma before and after them.

> He, *however*, did not submit his report on time.

**Noun**—a word that names a person, place, thing, quality, or action. It can function as subject of a verb, object of a verb and a preposition, and as an appositive.

**Objects**—nouns and pronouns which are "objects" of actions (verbs).

> She baked a cake. ("Cake" is the object created by the action of baking.)

**Parentheses** ( ) are used to separate explanations or qualifying statements within a sentence (each one of the curved lines is called a parenthesis). The part in the parentheses is called a parenthetical remark.

> My teenager (*like others his age*) thinks we adults know nothing.

**Parallel structure** is the term writers use to describe similar ideas expressed in similar form.

> Lin enjoys bik*ing*, hik*ing*, and swmm*ing*.

**Participles** are forms of verbs (verbals) that act as adjectives.

*Present participles* end in *–ing*

> *Having* brushed his teeth, Drew went to bed.

*Past participles* end in *–ed*

> *Exhausted*, Drew went to bed.

**Period** (.) is a punctuation mark that is placed at the end of complete sentences.

> Jody is a caring mother.

**Phrase**—a group of words that go together, but do not make a complete sentence.

> at home, in the morning, going home for the last time

**Preposition**—a word placed before a noun which is used to indicate position, direction, time, or some other abstract relationship (*at, to, for, against, from, with*, and *more*).

> *for* my grandchildren, *to* the store, *against* the wall, *at* nine o'clock

**Pronoun**—a word used in place of a noun (*he, she, him, her, they, them, it*).

> Ted plays the jazz trumpet; *he* is on tour.

**Pronoun/antecedent agreement** occurs when pronouns agree with their antecedents in number. A singular pronoun refers to a singular antecedent (see "Antecedent," above). A plural pronoun refers to a plural antecedent.

> A parent needs to be a good model for his or her (not "their") child.

**Pronoun case** tells the reader or listener whether the pronoun is naming:

- The *subject* of an action (called the *nominative* or *subjective* case pronouns: *he, she, we*)

  > *He* is an entrepreneur.

- The *receiver* or *object* of a verb or preposition (called the *objective* case pronouns: *him, her, us*)

  > Give *him* the file.

  > Give the file to *him*.

- The *owner* of something in the sentence (called the *possessive* case pronouns: *his, hers, ours*)

  > It is *his* file.

**Pronoun reference error**—When a pronoun lacks a clear and explicit antecedent, you have a pronoun reference error.

> After interviewing for several positions, I realized that *it* was not the career for me.

**Double quotation marks** (" ") are punctuation marks that enclose quotations.

> Patrick Henry exclaimed, **"**Give me liberty or give me death!**"**

**Reflexive pronoun**—a word that "reflects back" to the subject. It ends in "-self" (singular) or "-selves" (plural) and is used as object of prepositions and verbs. It *cannot* be removed from the sentence. (Compare with "intensive pronoun.")

> He did the work by *himself.* (Object of the preposition "by.")

> He did *himself* a favor. (Object of the verb "did.")

**Run-on (fused) sentence**—This occurs when two or more sentences "collide" or become "fused" because there is no punctuation between them.

> I like classical music  Beethoven is my favorite composer.
> --------sentence-------  ----------------sentence----------------

**Semicolon** (;)—There are three uses for the semicolon:

1. To join two independent clauses (complete sentences) that are closely related.

2. To join two independent clauses when the second clause begins with a conjunctive adverb (therefore, however, as a result, in fact, and more.)

3. To separate items in a series when one or more of the items contains a comma.

**Sentence**—It is also called an independent clause. It contains a subject and a verb and expresses a complete thought.

> Rosemary makes delicious pasta dishes.
> (subject)  (verb)

**Sentence fragments** are not sentences because they do not make sense by themselves.

> Craig who is a loving father.

**Single quotation marks** (' ') indicate certain titles and quotations within quotations.

> "Billie Holiday's song 'Gloomy Sunday' was banned from radio play because its lyrics were about a suicide."

**Subject**—the noun or pronoun that, with all of its modifiers, usually precedes the verb.

> Melody and Dustin, who are nature lovers, enjoy the outdoors.
> (subjects)         (modifier)         (verb)

**Subject-verb agreement** is a grammatical rule that states that the verb must agree in number with its subject.

> Joseph and Anthony *are* (not "is") very smart children.

**Subjunctive mood**—a verb mood that suggests possibility, wish, and contrary-to-fact condition, as opposed to a fact.

> I wish I *was* rich man.

> I wish I *were* a rich man.

**Underlining or italics** are used for major works such as books, plays, pamphlets, long musical works, TV and radio programs, long poems, periodicals, published speeches, movies, videos, and works of visual art.

> *War and Peace* (or War and Peace) is a classic Russian novel.

**Verb**—a word used to express an *action* or *state of being*.

Bret *thinks* (action) carefully before he acts.

Bret *is* intelligent. (Bret is in the state of being intelligent.)

# Resources

When I review grammar rules, I normally check one or more of the following resources. There are plenty of books, so be sure to check them out for yourself to see which one meets your needs.

Aaron, Jane E. The Little Brown Compact Handbook with Exercises. Reading, Massachusetts: Longman, 2009.

> As the title suggests, this grammar book is compact. I usually go to this one first.

Hogue, Ann. The Essentials of English: A Writer's Handbook. New York: Longman, 2003.

> Contains useful reference lists.

Raimes, Ann. Keys for Writers. Boston, New York: Houghton Mifflin Company, 2010.

> This book contains handy formats for MLA, APA, CBE, and Chicago Style documentation.

Sabin, William A. The Gregg Reference Manual. New York: McGraw-Hill Irwin, 2005.

> For 40 years, this book has been the "granddady" of all grammar books. It is all-inclusive. This book is my authority. When all else fails, I go to this book.

# About the Author

Ron holds an M.F.A. from American University, Washington, D.C.

When Ron worked in Washington, D.C., he developed and conducted communication skills workshops for federal agencies. His programs included *Essentials of English*, *Report Writing*, *Constructive Conflict Resolution*, *Interpersonal Communications*, *Techniques of Negotiation*, and *Performance Appraisal: Counseling and Feedback*. For the latter, he served as a consultant for Time-Life video.

As a guest speaker, Ron has spoken at conferences and for organizations such as the Smithsonian, NASA, Federal Women's Program, and the Air Force.

As a journalist, he wrote a *Human Resources* column for the award-wining, nationwide publication *Government Computer News*. His column was voted "best column" by its readers.

In Tucson, Ron conducts interpersonal skills workshops for organizations such as Head Start, Federal Corrections, and the Adult Probation Education Office. Ron and his wife Jane also develop and conduct marriage workshops.

Currently, Ron teaches college classes in writing, literature, ethics, critical thinking, diversity, interpersonal communication, popular culture, film, and the humanities.

Also, as a corporate trainer, he develops and conducts customer service, writing, and interpersonal communication workshops.

His most recent workshop is entitled *Connecting with Others: Regaining the Lost Art of Conversation*.

# Afterword

Thank you for your interest in my book.

As you know from reading "The Shocking Lack of Good Grammar in Today's Workplace" and "The High Cost of Bad Grammar," writers need all the help they can get.

It is my sincere wish that this book will help you improve your writing. And, in turn, I hope you can help others improve their writing.

Although this book will help you improve your writing quickly, improving it is not an overnight process. It takes time, patience, persistence, and effort. But it is well worth it!

My objective with this book is help you improve your writing in a concise and clear manner. Thus, if you have any suggestions as to how I can improve it, please contact me at the following website:

www.onechoicecanchangealife.com/authors/authormead.html.

Also, if you are interested in hosting a writing workshop, please contact me at meadtraining@comcast.net or at (520) 306-2057.

**Please remember:**

**Improving your writing is a journey, not a destination. So, enjoy your journey!**

Blessings,

CPSIA information can be obtained at www.ICGtesting.com
Printed in the USA
BVOW03s1206231114

375799BV00016B/365/P

9 781935 354222